CW01669690

THOMAS & FRIENDS

Overnight Stop

Based on a story by **Niki Lytton**
Adapted by **Ellen Philpott**

DEAN

First published in Great Britain 2024 by DEAN, part of Farshore
An imprint of HarperCollins*Publishers*
1 London Bridge Street, London SE1 9GF
www.farshore.co.uk

HarperCollins*Publishers*
Macken House, 39/40 Mayor Street Upper,
Dublin 1, D01 C9W8, Ireland

Based on a story by Niki Lytton
Adapted by Ellen Philpott

Based on the Railway Series by The Reverend W Awdry.

ISBN 978 0 00 870678 4
Printed in China
001

A CIP catalogue record for this title is available from the British Library.

It was sunrise at Tidmouth sheds. The trains were sleeping peacefully.

Just then, a loud whistle rang out, letting them know it was time to rise and shine. Thomas and Nia came rolling out of the sheds, raring to go.

18
1

Percy needed a little longer to get ready.
He was feeling very cosy this morning.

"Night light – off. Fan – off. Wheels – brushed. Now everything is Percy Perfect!" said Percy, as he zoomed after his friends.

Gordon was waiting at Knapford Station with nine tanker cars.

"Wow," said Thomas, "this looks like a really big job!"

"It is," said Gordon. "These tanker cars need to go all the way to Wayland."

"On the mainland? ***CHOO-HOO!***" said Nia. "I'm so in!"

1
18

"The mainland is a long way away ... We'll have to stay overnight!" said Thomas, bouncing around excitedly. "We get to camp out!"

As Nia and Thomas laughed and chatted, they didn't notice that poor Percy was not looking happy at all. He had never stayed away overnight before.

They were soon chugging across the countryside. But Percy was lagging behind, as he had packed an extra car with his fan, night light and all his other things from home. He had so many supplies that he was struggling to pull them along!

"If we're prepared, we won't be scared!" Percy told the others.

"Why would we be scared?" asked Nia, confused.

"Erm ... I thought one of you might feel nervous about camping out," Percy spluttered.

"Aw, thanks, Percy! But we're fine!" peeped Thomas.

As Percy rolled over a bump in the track, he didn't notice that his supply car had come unhooked!

"Look, it's the bridge to the mainland!" called Nia. "Last one across is a rusty rail spike!"

The engines raced across the bridge, full of excitement. But when Percy looked back, he was horrified to see that his supply car was gone.

"Oh, no! We have to turn back!" he pleaded.

"It's too late to turn back now!" said Thomas cheerfully.

6
1

At last, the three friends rolled into the woods for their overnight stop. The stars were twinkling above them. Nia and Thomas were thrilled to be camping out.

Just then, a wolf howled and Percy jumped in fright.

"I'm afraid to sleep away from home!" he cried, squeezing his eyes shut.

"Why didn't you tell us before?" asked Thomas.

"I didn't want you to think I was a scaredy-train," said Percy sadly.

"We are going to have so much fun, you'll forget about being scared," said Thomas.

And they did have lots of fun! They chased fireflies, told stories around the campfire, and looked at the stars.

"I think I'm starting to enjoy camping," Percy laughed.

"We should rest," said Thomas.
"We've got a lot of work to do tomorrow."

As they settled down to sleep, Percy thought about his cosy shed back on Sodor, with all his special things. It felt odd to be so far away from home.

Thomas and Nia soon peacefully fell asleep. But poor Percy just couldn't relax. Every time he closed his eyes, scary noises would jolt him awake. Owls hooted, leaves rustled and frogs croaked. It was all so strange!

"Thomas," Percy whispered. But Thomas didn't wake up.

"THOMAS!" Percy shouted.

"What's going on?" asked Thomas.

"Oh, you're awake!" said Percy.

"I am now!" laughed Thomas.

"There are so many funny noises," Percy complained.

Thomas tried to make Percy feel better. "When the crickets chirp, they sound a bit like train wheels creaking by at home," Thomas said.

HOO! HOO! An owl hooted above them.

"When the owl says '***HOO***,' it sounds like Gordon saying, 'Who moved my cargo?'" Thomas added.

"That's like home too." Percy giggled.

But then he let out a sad whistle.

"It's not like home at all," Percy sighed, then hid in a cloud of his steam.

The whistle had woken Nia up. "What's going on?" she said sleepily.

"I can't sleep here!" Percy exclaimed. "Everything is too different. I miss the shed, and I miss my cloud poster, and my nightlight and my fan ... And I don't know where to put my lucky bell!"

Nia and Thomas felt so sorry for him.

"I know," said Thomas. "If you can't be at home, then we are going to bring home to you."

Percy looked at Thomas in surprise. How could he do that?

Thomas found a canopy of trees for Percy to rest under while he slept, just like a shed roof.

Nia cleverly made a night light for Percy by softly shining her lights through a big leaf.

Next, Thomas puffed some clouds of smoke gently around Percy's head ... just like his cloud poster!

They set up Percy's bell in the same position as he had it at home, and then Thomas zoomed back and forth to make a gentle breeze, just like Percy's fan. At last, Percy's eyes started to droop, and he fell into a deep, peaceful sleep.

The next morning, Thomas zoomed over to Percy.

“You did it! You slept a whole night away from home!” he said.

“I did?” said Percy, waking up. “I really did!”

TING, TING! Percy's bell rang out as he brushed up his wheels, ready for the day ahead.

"I feel fit as a freight train, thanks to you two," Percy peeped happily. "Full steam ahead!"

"Let's not waste any time," said Thomas happily.

"And let's get a ***CHUG CHUG*** ..." started Nia.

"A ***CHUG CHUG*** ..." continued Thomas.

"A ***CHOO-CHOOING***!" finished Percy.

They tooted their horns as they raced onwards.